CHOOSE LOVE

"I'VE DECIDED TO STICK WITH LOVE." DR. MARTIN LUTHER KING, J.R.

Xulon Press
2301 Lucien Way #415
Maitland, FL 32751
407.339.4217
www.xulonpress.com

Paperback ISBN-13: 978-1-6628-6502-2
Ebook ISBN-13: 978-1-6628-6503-9

HELLO! MY NAME IS THEO AND THIS IS MY PERSON.
I WOULD LOVE TO KNOW, WHAT IS YOUR NAME?

I LOVE TO TAKE MY PERSON ON VISITS TO HEALTH CLINICS IN OUR COMMUNITY.
DO YOU HAVE DOGS WHO MAKE VISITS TO HEALTH CLINICS IN YOUR COMMUNITY?

BEFORE WE GO TO CLINICS, I HAVE A BATH SO I CAN BE
FRESH AND CLEAN FOR VISITS!

HAVE YOU EVER HAD A VISIT WITH A DOG AT A MEDICAL APPOINTMENT?

ON THE WAY TO THE CLINIC, I TAKE MY PERSON TO THE PARK AND
PLAY FETCH.

SHARING MY BALL AT THE PARK IS MY FAVORITE GAME!
WHAT IS YOUR FAVORITE GAME?

I GET VERY EXCITED WALKING INTO OUR CLINIC!

I JUMP HIGH, SPIN AROUND, AND LOOK FOR ANYONE WANTING A VISIT!

I SEE SOMEONE FEELING ANGRY.

I LOVE THEM BY SHARING PATIENCE.

I FEEL ANGRY WHEN MY BROTHER TAKES MY BALL AWAY!

IT IS HELPFUL TO ME DURING ANGRY TIMES WHEN MY PERSON GIVES ME A CHEW TOY.

WHEN WAS THE LAST TIME YOU FELT ANGER?

WHAT HELPS YOU WHEN YOU FEEL ANGRY?

THE NEXT PERSON I SEE IS FEELING GRIEF,

I LOVE THEM BY SHARING HOPE.

I FELT GRIEF WHEN MY DOG FRIEND MOVED TO A DIFFERENT STATE.

IT HELPS ME WHEN I CALL MY DOG FRIEND ON THE PHONE!

HAVE YOU EVER FELT GRIEF?

WHAT HELPED YOU?

NOW I SEE A PERSON FEELING LONELY.

I LOVE THEM BY SHARING TIME!

I FEEL LONELY WHEN I CAN'T RUN ERRANDS WITH MY PERSON.

IT HELPS ME WHEN I SEE HER WALK BACK THROUGH OUR DOOR!

DO YOU EVER FEEL LONELY?

WHAT HELPS YOU WHEN YOU FEEL ALONE?

WE'VE ALL HAD TIMES WHEN WE'VE FELT SAD.

I CHOOSE TO LOVE OTHERS.

IT TURNS SADNESS INTO GLADNESS!

I FEEL SAD AND DISAPPOINTMENT WHEN I CAN'T BARK AT VISITORS
IN OUR HOME.

DOING TRICKS FOR OUR VISITORS TURNS MY SADNESS INTO GLADNESS!

WHEN WAS THE LAST TIME YOU FELT SAD?

WHAT HELPS YOU EXCHANGE SADNESS FOR GLADNESS?

I'VE SPENT SO MUCH TIME LOVING OTHERS,
I FEEL NOW IS A GOOD TIME TO TAKE A BREAK.

HOW DO YOU FEEL WHEN YOU NEED A BREAK?
WHAT HELPS YOU FEEL RESTED AND LOVED?
HOW DO YOU FEEL AFTER RESTING?

I WILL TAKE MY PERSON BACK TO THE PARK AND PLAY FETCH.

SHARING MY BALL AT THE PARK MAKES ME FEEL LOVED!

THANK YOU FOR SHARING YOUR TIME WITH US!

I FEEL HAPPY WHEN I SPEND TIME WITH YOU SHARING MY STORY OF OUR VISITS IN OUR WONDERFUL COMMUNITY!

IF YOU WOULD LIKE TO BECOME A
CERTIFIED ANIMAL ASSISTED THERAPY TEAM
WITH YOUR DOG
PLEASE VISIT
WWW.THERAPYDOGS.COM

IF YOU WOULD LIKE TO SEE MORE OF THEO DURING HIS THERAPY TIMES,
PLEASE REACH OUT TO US ON
FACEBOOK AT PUBLICATIONS BY GENICE FULTON
OR ON
INSTAGRAM AT
PUBLICATIONS_BYGENICEFULTON
OR SCAN THE CODE ON THE NEXT PAGE!

THEOSTHERAPYTIMES

ONE OF GENICE'S FAVORITE AAT MEMORIES IS A LITTLE GIRL WHO WAS FOUR YEARS OLD. HER MOM HAD DRESSED HER IN A BEAUTIFUL SUMMER DRESS WITH MATCHING SANDALS. THIS LITTLE GIRL HAD CURLY, LONG, DARK FLOWING HAIR, AND BIG BROWN EYES. SHE WAS ALMOST PICTURE PERFECT WITH HER GOLD EARRINGS, BRACELET, & MATCHING HAIR BARRETTE. AS THEO APPROACHED HER, GENICE COULD SEE BIG TEARS FALLING DOWN HER LITTLE ROUND CHEEKS.

THEO SLOWED HIS PACE AND GENTLY WALKED TOWARD HER. THEO STOPPED ABOUT A FOOT AWAY FROM HER WHILE HE KEPT EYE CONTACT WITH HER. SHE RAN TO THEO, WRAPPED HER ARMS AROUND HIM AND REPEATEDLY KISSED THE TOP OF HIS FLUFFY HEAD AS BIG TEARS QUIETLY CONTINUED DOWN HER FACE. GENICE SOFTLY ASKED, "ARE YOU OKAY?" BUT SHE REFUSED TO RESPOND TO ANYONE EXCEPT THEO. HER MOM EXPLAINED SHE HAD EXPERIENCED MANY NEEDLES THAT DAY DURING HER MEDICAL TREATMENT AND WAS ANGRY WITH ALL ADULTS. GENICE KEPT QUIET AND DECIDED TO SIT ON THE FLOOR AND WAIT. AFTER SEVERAL MINUTES, THE TEARS STOPPED AND A SMILE CAME ACROSS HER SWEET LITTLE FACE AS HER EYES LIT UP.

HER MOM ASKED IF SHE FELT BETTER. SHE SMILED REALLY BIG AND SAID, "YES!" AS SHE SKIPPED OVER TO HER MOM AND PLACED HER HAND IN HER MOM'S HAND. AS SHE WAS WALKING AWAY WITH HER MOM, SHE TURNED WITH A HUGE SMILE, WAVED GOODBYE TO THEO AND BLEW HIM A KISS!

ANOTHER FAVORITE MEMORY IS A VISIT IN PEDIATRIC DENTAL. GENICE ASKED A LITTLE BOY IF HE WOULD LIKE TO PET THEO. HE COULDN'T SPEAK BECAUSE HE HAD TEETH EXTRACTED ON BOTH SIDES OF HIS MOUTH. HIS MOUTH WAS FULL OF GAUZE BUT HE GRINNED EAR TO EAR WITH HIS SWEET LITTLE GAUZE SMILE AND HIS EYES LIT UP WHEN THEO WALKED OVER TO HIM FOR A BIG HUG AND A HIGH FIVE!

GENICE HAS SO MANY FAVORITE AAT MEMORIES, SHE COULD KEEP RECALLING THEM ALL DAY! FOR EXAMPLE, THERE WAS THE DAY THEO SHOWED SPECIAL ATTENTION TO AN ADULT. AT FIRST, SHE WAS HESITANT TO PET THEO. THEO LOVES BACK SCRATCHES. HE WALKED UP TO HER AND TURNED HIS BACK TO HER. AS SHE SCRATCHED HIS BACK, SHE STARTED LAUGHING. THEO WAS INTRIGUED BY HER INFECTIOUS LAUGHTER. AS SHE LAUGHED, THEO BEGAN JUMPING STRAIGHT UP IN THE AIR! SHE EXCLAIMED, "OH! THEO LOVES EVERYBODY!" EVERYONE IN THE CLINIC WAS LAUGHING AT THEM TOGETHER!

ALSO A FAVORITE IS MAKING PEOPLE LAUGH WHEN THEO DOES HIS TRICKS DURING VISITS! THEO IS A CERTIFIED TRICK DOG AND LOVES TO ENTERTAIN DURING HIS VISITS! PATIENTS, STAFF, & CAREGIVERS GATHER TOGETHER AS THEO JUMPS THROUGH HIS HOOP, SPINS IN CIRCLES, WAVES HELLO, AND GIVES EVERYONE A HIGH FIVE! THEO'S FAVORITE IS POSING FOR PHOTOS WITH HIS FANS!

THIS BOOK'S CREATOR, GENICE AND HER RESCUE DOG BO, WE'RE AN ANIMAL ASSISTED THERAPY TEAM AT A
LONG TERM CARE FACILITY IN HILO HAWAI'I IN 2010.

BUT GENICE DIDN'T UNDERSTAND THE FULL IMPACT OF THEIR VISITS UNTIL
SHE UNEXPECTEDLY FOUND HERSELF ON THE OTHER SIDE OF ANIMAL ASSISTED THERAPY IN 2021.
IN JULY OF THAT YEAR HER GRANDDAUGHTER, EDEN, HAD TO UNDERGO BRAIN SURGERY
& WAS VISITED BY RUBY, THE AAT DOG FOR ASSISTANCE DOGS OF HAWAI'I.
IT WAS DURING THAT STORM OF LIFE THAT GENICE DISCOVERED
ANIMAL ASSISTED THERAPY (AAT) IS WHAT SHE WAS CREATED TO DO!

CURRENTLY, GENICE AND HER RE-HOMED DOGS, THEO & AUGUSTUS, MAKE AAT VISITS TO
COMMUNITY HEALTH CLINICS, DRUG REHAB FACILITIES, LONG TERM CARE FACILITIES, ASSISTED LIVING FACILITIES, AND
HOSPITALS SPECIALIZING IN SERIOUS MEDICAL ILLNESS, TRAUMA, & INTENSIVE CARE.
THEY ACCEPT OTHER INVITATIONS REQUESTING AAT.

GENICE, THEO, & AUGUSTUS CONSIDER IT A GREAT HONOR AND PRIVILEGE
TO SPEND TIME WITH THE AMAZING PEOPLE IN THEIR COMMUNITY.

TO READ MORE ABOUT HOW,
"THEO'S THERAPY TIMES"
CAME TO LIFE,
PLEASE VISIT US AT:

FACEBOOK @ PUBLICATIONS BY GENICE FULTON
OR
INSTAGRAM @ PUBLICATIONS_BYGENICEFULTON

INTERESTING TIDBITS FROM AAT WEBSITES!

ALLIANCE OF THERAPY DOGS
"ACCORDING TO THE AMERICAN VETERINARY MEDICAL ASSOCIATION (AVMA),
ANIMAL ASSISTED THERAPY OR ANIMAL ASSISTED ACTIVITIES",
"PROVIDE OPPORTUNITIES FOR MOTIVATION, EDUCATION,
"ARE AN INTEGRAL PART OF THE TREATMENT PROCESS",
"MEANT TO IMPROVE THE PHYSICAL, SOCIAL, EMOTIONAL, AND COGNITIVE FUNCTIONS OF HUMANS",
"AAT DATES BACK TO ANCIENT GREECE",
"MEDICAL PROVIDERS AND THERAPISTS WHO SUPPORT AAT BELIEVE IT HAS MANY BENEFITS SUCH AS
HELPING WITH PERSONAL AND SOCIAL DEVELOPMENT, INCREASED SELF-ESTEEM, IMPROVED MENTAL
HEALTH, BETTER SOCIAL SKILLS, AND INCREASED EMPATHY AND NURTURING SKILLS",
THERAPY IS PROVIDED "IN MANY SETTINGS, INCLUDING BUT NOTHING LIMITED TO AIRPORTS, NURSING
HOMES, ASSISTED LIVING FACILITIES, REHAB FACILITIES, MENTAL HEALTH INSTITUTIONS, SCHOOLS,
HOSPITALS, CANCER CENTERS, HOSPICE FACILITIES, COLLEGE CAMPUSES", "IN PATIENTS' HOMES".

FOR MORE INFORMATION, PLEASE VISIT THEIR WEBSITE AT
WWW.THERAPYDOGS.COM

SUNSHINE THERAPY ANIMALS
"STUDIES SHOW PHYSICAL CONTACT WITH AN ANIMAL LOWERS BLOOD PRESSURE, DECREASES
CHOLESTEROL LEVELS, REDUCES ANXIETY, BOOSTS THE IMMUNE SYSTEM, DECREASES AGGRESSION AND
INCREASES SOCIALIZATION AND COMMUNICATION."

FOR MORE INFORMATION, PLEASE VISIT THEIR WEBSITE AT
WWW.LAPANSUNSHINEFOUNDATION.ORG/ABOUT-SUNSHINE-THERAPY-ANIMALS
OR ON INSTAGRAM AT
SUNNYS PETS TUCSON

IN A PROJECT LIKE THIS, THERE ARE ALWAYS SO MANY TO THANK!
THIS BOOK IS DEDICATED TO:

ALL THE ANIMAL ASSISTED THERAPY TEAMS...PAST, CURRENT, & FUTURE,
AND ESPECIALLY THOSE WHO BLAZED THE TRAIL BEFORE US!

MY FAMILY & FRIENDS, THANK YOU FOR YOUR LOVE AND ENCOURAGEMENT TO CHASE MY DREAMS!

MIKE, THANK YOU FOR SUPPORTING AND NUDGING ME ALONG MY PATH FOR THE PAST 27+ YEARS!

MY BESTIE, WHO HAS BELIEVED IN ME FOR ALMOST 40 YEARS,
ENDURING COUNTLESS HOURS
OF LISTENING TO MY RAMBLINGS
SO I COULD GET STORIES OUT OF MY HEART
AND ON PAPER!

THEO,
THANK YOU FOR TEACHING ME
THE TRUE LESSON OF
"AT MY FEET".

OUR SUNSHINE THERAPY ANIMAL TEAM. YOU'RE THE MOST AMAZING ORGANIZATION, TRULY PUTTING THE
"RUBBER TO THE ROAD" FOR TUCSON AND I'M SO GRATEFUL TO BE A PART OF OUR GROUP!

CINDY MORGAN, THANK YOU FOR HAVING MULTIPLE SOLUTIONS TO ALL MY MANY QUESTIONS. AND THANKS
FOR GIVING ME THE KICK IN THE PANTS REQUIRED TO FINISH THIS BOOK!

AND TO OUR AMAZING TUCSON COMMUNITY,
WE WILL NEVER FORGET HOW YOU SO READILY ACCEPT, AND LOOK FORWARD TO OUR VISITS!
THANK YOU!

"TO KNOW EVEN ONE LIFE HAS BREATHED EASIER BECAUSE YOU HAVE LIVED.
THIS IS TO HAVE SUCCEEDED."
RALPH WALDO EMERSON